Testimonials

"Each and every piece of advice Joshua gave me was worth gold. He constantly advised and actioned in my best interest and made it possible for me to sell my property and buy a house of my choice. I did not experience the same with any other agency within the whole of the area. He is a true expert and professional and no one knows the area better then him. I would give ten stars if I could, not five."

– RK, local vendor

"Joshua is an excellent customer focussed individual and always ensures professionalism coupled with the zeal to walk that extra mile. We are very comfortable dealing with him as his skills are immaculate. My wife and I were very impressed."

– Arjun Chakladar, local vendor

"I had the pleasure of working with Joshua Glanville. He is one of a kind. Very responsive and easily reachable whenever I had any concerns or questions. Also very approachable and friendly treating each case individually. Overall I am satisfied with the services I received and would highly recommend his expertise to anyone."

– GS, local buyer

The Future is Now:

Top tips for selling your property in tomorrow's market today!

By Joshua Glanville

Please read the following Disclaimers

No promises or guarantees are offered or intended. The tips in this book are anecdotal, based on personal experience, and on experiences of friends/colleagues of the author. They are offered purely to give ideas. Professional advice should be taken before carrying out any building, conveyancing, sales or investments. The tips within should not be interpreted as advice as past performance is no indication of the future. Investment values can go down, as well as up, and sums invested in property may diminish in value. Legislation, property, and planning laws are ever changing. Professional advice from appropriate bodies including, but not limited to, solicitors, building control, planning departments, surveyors, accountants and tax advisors should be sought before investing any monies or purchasing/disposing of any asset. The author accepts no liability for any tips offered within these pages and the reader accepts full responsibility to take appropriate advice before making any decisions regarding their property.

The material in this publication is of the nature of GENERAL comment only and DOES NOT represent PROFESSIONAL ADVICE. It is not intended to provide specific guidance for particular circumstances and it should not be relied upon as the basis for any decision to take action, or not take action, on any matter which it covers. Readers should obtain professional advice, where appropriate, before making any such decision. To the maximum extent permitted by law, the authors and publisher disclaim all responsibility and liability to any person arising directly or indirectly from any person taking or not taking action based on the information in this publication.

First Edition 2020

Acknowledgements

A huge thank you to everyone involved with making this book
happen, including my Mum and my amazing mentor Lisa B who
this wouldn't have been possible without.

I wouldn't be where I am today without the support of both of my
parents, through the lowest lows and the highest highs they've
always stood by me and supported my dreams, no matter how ludi-
crous they may have seemed at the time.

Thank you to Noura who gave me a chance and persevered with
me (even when I couldn't drive!). The best boss I ever had!

Lisa, you took my foundations as an agent and turned them into
a full-on, luxury skyscraper. Thank you for taking me under your
wing – the only way is up!

Bonus

If you're reading this, there's a strong chance it's because you're interested in selling your house, so let me tell you a bit about what we can offer you.*

We operate on a no-sale-no-fee basis, so if we fail to sell your property, you don't pay us! It's as simple as that, meaning there is no risk on your back.

We like to refer to ourselves as a 'cloud-based agent'. In simple terms, this means we are based online, and can market your property online using cutting edge marketing techniques all over the internet, to help your property reach a bigger audience, hence increasing your chances of a quick and attractive sale. This is the future of estate agency, and gives you a big advantage over your competition. Your competition is of course, other homes on the market at the same time as you.

Your property will also be marketed on the standard property portals, such as Rightmove and Zoopla, so what

*Only applies for relevant areas. We cover West London, so if your property is in Leeds, Liverpool, or anywhere outside of London, I'm afraid this doesn't apply for you.

we're offering includes what your typical high street agent offers, but so so much more. This is a unique approach that is simply not being used in the UK, and will really make your property stand out. Most agents will list a property on the portals, put a 'For Sale' board outside your house, and call a few people on their database. We do all of this, but have a plethora of other methods to attract buyers as well. Your property is the honey, and we are the expert to find you plenty of bees.

Give us a call for a FREE valuation of your property, to talk about our services, or if you would like any advice related to the property market at all. You can find our contact details at the end of the book, so please get in touch!

As a special offer for my readers, I'm offering a free marketing consultation, and a free marketing video if you list your property with us.

Simply quote the code: JG1000 to redeem this offer.

Contents

66

90% of all millionaires become so through owning real estate

- Andrew Carnegie

Introduction

I WAS BORN INTO a family of property developers. At an early age, on Sunday Mornings, I would climb into bed with my parents, who would have the Sunday newspaper property sections spread enticingly over their bed – 'property porn', as they would call it. Friends were always calling my Mum for property advice, and she seemed to know every property that was on the market in West London. I either had to grow up hating real estate or loving it, and fortunately for you, dear reader, I loved it. By the age of ten I would be scouring local papers for deals, and I remember finding one particularly amazing property deal which we ended up buying. I was rewarded with a new 'Pop Party' CD, which, looking back on it now, seems a bit mean!

The family business spanned the South of Italy and the whole of London. In many ways these worlds could not be more different. In Italy we would often pay for services with olive oil and oranges from our land. Greasing the right palms with our extra extra virgin oil was a great way of sourcing deals, and we picked up some amazing properties along the way, from tiny trulli (little witch-hat shaped houses) to a magnificent mansion with its own church, which is still in the family today. What was not so easy was selling these properties. The local Italian towns had as many high street agents as you'd find in the UK, but spotting them was as hard as finding a prized Italian truffle without a pig – you had to look hard to spot their presence. They would normally have a few photocopied sheets of A4 copy in the window, a couple of which might be accompanied by a photo or two if you were lucky. When you went inside to ask for details, you would either be met by a locked door (they really take advantage of their siestas in Puglia), or you would be handed a photocopy of a rough address, and an estimate of land size. As a result, properties could sit unsold for years, and one had to become pretty creative to even get a viewing. This actually served us well. Luckily for my parents, at this time I was also developing a bit of a passion for the internet. I built websites, I blasted social media, and I mastered search engine optimisation until our properties were the first thing you saw when you searched for a holiday home in Italy. 'Build it, and they will come' … and come they did! By breaking the mould and having a little imagination, we had enquiries from potential buyers all over the planet. I even ran a competition to sell one of our properties.

Back in London you would have thought that things would be a little more state-of-the-art when it came to property selling, but in truth I did not see an awful lot of difference. Most agents were getting listings, putting photos in their windows, and passively riding the property wave. In time, online portals like Rightmove and Zoopla made their jobs even easier. List it online and the buyers will come. Whaaaaaaat!?!? Seriously, how can that 'service' be worth 2% of the value of the most important asset most people will ever own? While the markets were booming, sellers barely noticed or cared as every property would have multiple offers, and gazumping was rife. But what to do when things go a little pear shaped? Bubbles, Brexit and big fat pandemics have made buyers sit up and realise that they have a lot more power and could negotiate big fat discounts off the asking price. So what did British estate agents do to accommodate this change? … ummm … nothing. They have carried on photocopying, listing online, and waiting for buyers to find them.

I found this a little crazy to be honest. I had seen what a difference a little bit of interactive internet promotion had made with our Italian empire, and could hardly believe how agents were still using the same techniques they had been using for decades, even in a rapidly slowing market. This was a bit of a double edged sword for me. On one hand it meant that I could jump on the property ladder and pick up some crazy bargains, buying my first deal when I was just seventeen. I had to set up a trust and get a loan from parents and grandparents and aunties and their cats, but I managed to scrape together £353,000 to buy my first investment. I moved in, rolled up my sleeves, found an affordable team of Polish builders to help me move a few walls, put in a new kitchen and bathroom etc. I ended up spending about £25,000 in all. I was eighteen years old now, and had my own luxury pad in West London. Sadly, parents, grandparents, aunties and their cats soon started to ask when they were going to get their money back. I had hoped to get a mortgage, but as an eighteen year old school leaver this was not going to be easy. I decided to test out my selling skills. I dressed the place and I blasted the market. I pushed on social media and told everyone I could think of about this amazing property that was up for grabs. I ended up selling the property for £570,000, making nearly £175,000. I was debt free, and on fire at the age of eighteen. I moved back home and plotted world real estate domination.

Around the time that I bought that first property, I was working at Metro Bank, the UK's number one challenger bank. I knew that banking was not for me but I LOVED how this company thought outside the box. We were told that we were not after new customers, we were looking for 'raving fans'. We had stores, not branches. We had magic money machines for kids (long before Jeremy Corbyn took over that phrase!). We had free dog biscuits for our four-legged friends. They were little things, but they created raving fans, and Metro soon became the fastest growing UK challenger bank. I learned a lot about customer management at this time, and how business is all about falling in love with your customer, not your product. The customer is always evolving and multi-faceted. The service has to follow them, not the other way around. Bringing this back to real estate, this is so relevant. One particular high street agent shook up the estate agency industry in the 2000s. They had trendy new shops serving perrier water, with shiny digital screens displaying properties. Nice! But did they really fall in love with their customers? These tiny tweaks set them apart from the other agencies, whose model was still stuck in the 80s, but how much of it was gimmick and how much of it was truly serving the customer? Their profits are now a fraction of what they once were. At the end of the day, their brand may have been sexier, but they were still working an old model, albeit in a shinier package.

Were they building raving fans? Did they utilise all of the resources that were out there? On the contrary, they have been on the receiving end of a lot of bad press due to their high fees, the way they treat their staff, and even an Office of Fair Trading investigation. My point here is not to put down any particular agency. To be honest, estate agents do not have a great reputation with or without my input, but that is a very British thing. It is about time that we, as agents, earned our commission and made the public fall in love with us again!

Whilst at Metro Bank, I knew that property was the way forward for me – I wanted to live and breathe it. I wanted to own it, develop it, sell it, and help others to sell, own and develop, so I went and joined the top family-owned local estate agency as a sales and lettings negotiator in my area. They trained me very well, for which I will be eternally grateful, and I made it my mission to create raving fans. Within two months, I was regularly achieving the top sales figures in the whole company. In my last nine months for that company I brought in 20% of their entire revenue across all four offices. I was also awarded the title of the 'One to Watch' in 2017, whilst I kept being named 'Sales Negotiator Of The Month' and 'Lettings Negotiator Of The Month' throughout my time at the company. To put this into context, this was at a time when my colleagues were being completely flummoxed by buyer reticence around Brexit.

So how did I do it? I thought outside the box. I created raving fans in my buyers who repeatedly left me five-star reviews online. I would sneakily advertise properties on Facebook, until I was asked to take them down by the owner of the business as it wasn't his style. I never understood this. It was such an easy way to reach our potential buyers, and it worked! Everyone has a phone these days and how many hours do we spend gazing at social media? Why wouldn't we be cashing in on that? This has been the secret to my success. People see my face all over the internet. They see me, they see the properties I am selling, and you can guess what happens next....

I loved selling houses, I really did, but I knew that I couldn't stay working under the old fashioned high street estate agency model. It felt like I was living in the 1980s. I travelled to Sydney, the Gold Coast, and Florida, and immersed myself in real estate for several months. Australia and the USA have a very different selling system whereby property is sold by qualified, self employed real estate agents. These people have to train and become legally qualified before they can sell property, while in the UK anyone can put up a sign and call themselves an agent. Furthermore, as self-employed realtors, our global colleagues have no guaranteed salary. If they don't sell, they don't get paid. This makes them HUNGRY and gets them off their backsides to do whatever it takes to get properties sold. They are Kings and Queens of marketing and social media, and you can bet your bottom dollar (Australian or American) that they will get you the best price possible for your home. An employed agent in the UK just wants a deal. They are in competition with the other agents in their agency, and they just want to get your home sold at any price. If they achieve an extra £20,000 for you, most agents will literally earn less than £15 more in commission. So why would they bother? This just doesn't happen in other countries.

I was bowled over by the marketing techniques I saw in Australia, where I met the international real estate marketing guru, Lisa B, who took me under her wing. She saw me as an excited puppy dog and she wanted to teach me all of her tricks. What Lisa doesn't know about selling houses is, frankly, not worth knowing. I came back from Australia and felt like Superman. Within a week, I had brokered a deal for one of our family properties that had been sticking on the market for TWO YEARS. And how did I do this? I just took a few photos and listed on Rightmove! Ummmm…..NO!!! I got a video camera and a drone, and I made an Oscar-worthy, somewhat humorous video about the property, and then I went online and I blasted LinkedIn. I made calls to anybody and everybody I could think of … I did what I had to do to get the job done like my life depended on it. I knew that I wanted to lead the UK into the 21st century and show them how it should be done, hence starting up my own agency.

My family's business model was to buy and flip. My grandparents and my great-grandparents were landlords, and my Mum swore that she would never make that mistake. I think this was a little harsh, but the point being that once a property was looking amazing, it was in our interests to get it sold FAST and to move on to the next project. We became masters of this.

People hesitate over the strangest things. You would think that buyers would have some imagination, and they do, but you have to give them a hand. If there is a funny smell in the kitchen, they will comment. It becomes 'the smelly house', 'the fishy house', 'the house with a floater in the loo' – yes, I have actually had that last one a couple of times. This shouldn't make a difference, but it does. Who wants to buy the house with the floater?! This is why I've collated my A-Z of top tips for sellers. I want my vendors to get the best price. I want to create a frenzy around your property. I want open houses where potential buyers are considering hitmen to knock out the competition!

My selling model is still based on creating raving fans. There are tiny details that can make the biggest difference, and there are also huge details that can make very little difference. When you sell a home, you are selling a dream – this is most people's biggest lifetime investment, so they need to get excited and fall in love a little. My Mum is the most canny person I know in real estate, but she admits to buying her first home because it smelled like apples and cinnamon!

I never approach two properties in the same way. Some properties almost sell themselves, but if it's already a fabulous property then I need to get out there and get an even more fabulous price. Some properties have not been touched for generations, and are perfect for developers who really don't care about a shiny white kitchen as they intend to turn the place into a block of flats anyway, whilst some buyers prefer to buy a property which needs updating/something they can add value to. It is my job to identify the potential, to fall in love with your property, and to understand who else I can get to fall in love with it at the best price. I liaise with my sellers to form a cunning plan in order to help them achieve this.

The following is my A-Z of top tips to sell your home for the best price. Some may seem obvious, but that doesn't necessarily mean that they are always done. Go on Airbnb – will you book the place with the unironed duvet and scratchy towels, or will you opt for the exact same property next door that has the crisp white linens and scented candles? It isn't rocket science, but it all helps to seduce the buyer. The list is pretty comprehensive and you can dip in and out. Some are absolute red light, don't even think about going to market until this is done, 'musts'. Sometimes you can have the green light to go to market but a property just isn't getting the offers it deserves. That is when the green light tips might come into their own.

I truly love my job. I love making sellers' dreams come true when we get a great price for their most valuable asset. I love making buyers' dreams come true, whether they are investors who I am setting up with building teams on their first venture, or people falling in love with their next home. I just love property. I love seeing the potential, I love seeing the amazing things people do with their homes, and the exciting developments in 21st century building materials and archi-tecture. This is my passion and my life. I am thrilled to share some of this knowledge with you and hope that my tips can help you to achieve an outstanding price for your home. My vision for estate agency is current, forward thinking, and it works!

Now, this book is specifically targeted at sellers, and how you can put yourself in the best possible position to sell your house, however all sellers do become buyers at some point. If you would like any advice on buying, how to spot a deal, and the best general approaches to purchasing a property, then please get in touch and I will be happy to support/guide you through the process to finding your dream home.

Some people look for a beautiful place, others make a place beautiful

- Hazrat Inayat Khan

The Traffic Light System

I T IS WORTH noting that not everything in this A-Z will be essential. There will be some things that are hugely important, and some that you don't particularly NEED to do, but might seriously help you out if you did. For this reason, I've created a traffic light system to help you understand which topics have what level of importance.

This traffic light system is for residential sales, and does not necessarily apply if you are selling to developers. Developers will not care what colour your carpets are, or how pretty your scented candles are. Certain properties lend themselves well to developers, so if you think this may be your house, the best thing you can do is to chat to your agent and anticipate the demand by applying for appropriate planning permission. Your agent should also be able to identify this as part of your marketing action plan with them. The planning permission is only an option – buyers can take it or leave it, but it opens up possibilities for them and can pique developers' interest. I have even spoken with a couple of developers recently who have said that they won't buy a property that doesn't already have planning permission. If you are aiming at both end user/home owner, and developer, then read on, and keep all doors open.

● **RED:** Highly important. This is something that you MUST do before allowing viewings.

● **AMBER:** Medium level of importance. You could leave this out, but I'd highly recommend doing it for best results.

○ **GREEN:** You could comfortably go to the market without this, it's just a recommendation that can make a difference to the value of your house, and something that can reduce the level of buyer objections if it is sticking on the market.

● **(RED) Agency** – This is likely to be the longest chapter, because choosing the right agent is essential. It's the ultimate difference maker on how much you sell your property for, how quickly you're able to sell, and reducing your chances of everyone's worst nightmare: a fallthrough.

The first thing you need to consider when deciding on which agency to go with, is whether to choose an online agent, or a high street agent. High street agents have a physical office space which you can visit during working hours if you fancy a face-to-face chat. Having a physical office also offers exposure of your property to members of the public who happen to be walking down the street on any given day, but with high street retail being in huge decline this is much less relevant than it used to be. Working on the high street myself, I would quite regularly see people stopping by our window and having a browse at what was on the market, although very few of them would end up coming into the office to take any further action.

Something to consider is that high street agents get paid a vast percentage of their wage as a guaranteed salary. The commission that goes to the agency is high, but the commission that goes to the individual agent is minimal, which leaves agents chasing sales at any cost. Another £10,000 on the agreed price of your property might make a huge difference to you but make only a few pounds of difference to what the individual agent gets, so they aren't as hungry to negotiate. This can lead to less than satisfactory results and is one of the reasons agents can have a bad name.

Let's face it – high street agency is a very dated model. Very few people traipse from agent to agent looking at physical photocards and

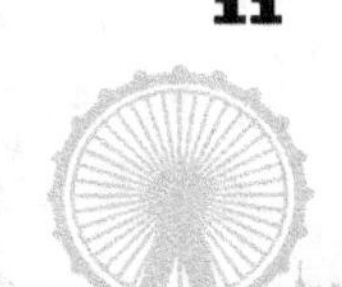

asking for paper brochures these days. Buyers are far more likely, in this day and age, to browse online.

Online agents don't tend to have any physical premises, which means that they are saving a lot of money from not having to pay any rent, which can really work to your advantage. The money that's being saved can and should be reinvested into the marketing of your property, increasing the reach of prospective buyers, and therefore increasing your chances of a prompt and lucrative sale.

It's worth noting that there are various types of online agency, one of which is the Purplebricks model, whereby the agent will charge an upfront fee which you lose whether or not they sell your property. This is the cheaper option, but I would advise against taking that approach. You have to question their motivation to put effort into selling the property if they've already got your money in the bag. Why bust a gut to get the best price, or even to get buyers through your door, when there is no further financial incentive? Other than the fact that they don't have physical premises, they generally operate similarly to a high street agent as they let the property sit on the likes of Rightmove and Zoopla without any additional marketing, and you have to pay extra if you want them to conduct the viewings for you. I've also found a lot of people complaining about their lack of support throughout the selling process, with minimal help when it comes to the legal process, thus increasing the chances of a fallthrough.

The other online approach is the self-employed agent model. This is the established model in countries like the USA and Australia, and is really taking off in the UK now for very good reasons. Here, you have highly motivated individual agents who, like high street agents, operate on a no-sale-no-fee basis. This leaves them highly motivated to a) get your property sold and b) at the best possible price. The money saved from the lack of physical premises can be invested into the marketing and promotion of your property to a much wider audience. Just like every other agent, they'll put your property on the popular property portals, such as Rightmove and Zoopla, but they are keen to go the extra mile, marketing all over social media and various other platforms. They'll stand by you every step of the way, chasing solicitors and guiding you through the entire process. The only way they can earn their living is by seeing your property all the way through to completion. If it falls through or doesn't sell, they don't get paid, so that extra motivation is there, making this a very attractive option for sellers.

Now that you've figured out which type of agent to use, you can make a shortlist of the best agents in your chosen category. For this, it's best to do some research online, ask other local people who they would recommend, look at the kind of properties the various agencies have on the market – including their general price range – and book in some valuations.

Fees are a natural talking point when you meet with an agent, and this is something you really have to think through. A large number of people decide which agent to go with, purely based on whoever is offering the lowest fee, which is why so many people have tried online agencies such as Purplebricks. But as already mentioned, what level of service are you going to get if you choose this option? The agent charging the higher fee may be costing you a few thousand pounds extra, but they're also more likely to achieve a higher price for you, which in turn makes that slightly higher fee redundant. There's a reason so many people switch to other agents after failing to sell through the online agents....

Fees in the UK normally work out at around 1-3% of the selling price, which is an absolute bargain compared to countries like the USA and Italy, whose fees nudge 6%. So, how does the 1% agent compare to the 3% agent? This is a hard one, and there is no simple answer. If the fee is too low then that may indicate that an agent is short of listings, and that could be for a good reason. A 3% agent may be so good that the extra 2% fee is easily absorbed in the 10% extra that they achieve in asking price, but this will not always be the case. My advice is to not make the fee your top reason for choosing an agent.... Go with your gut. How excited is the agent by your property? What resources do they plan to put into selling your property? What sets them apart? I would not advise that you over-negotiate the price down. If an agent is selling property A at 1% and property B at 3%, which do you think they will push their buyers towards? Your 2% saving might cost you your sale. Ultimately, you get what you pay for, so wait until you see what an amateur, who will generally charge a much lower fee, will cost you. If an agent can't negotiate their own fee, how are they going to be able to negotiate the best price for your property?

Now there's the value of your property, and this is something you need to be cautious of. Let's say your house is worth £800,000, and you have three agents who come round to value (you should always invite multiple agents to get a good idea of the true value). One values it at £850,000, one values it at £775,000, and the other values it at £800,000. Most people will automatically be drawn to the agent who valued it at £850,000, and I don't blame them in the slightest! It is human nature to be attracted to the bigger number. As a toddler my favourite number was 100 just because it was the biggest number I knew existed! But if an agent is overvaluing your property like this, the chances are very low that they can actually achieve that price. They are using a big number to reel you in and get you tied into their contract, but a week or two after listing, with minimal viewings, they'll ask you for a price reduction … and then another one … and another one, until it's down to £775,000. At this point they'll probably sell the property because it's now below the market value, they'll get their commission, and they're happy, while you're left with a sale price far lower than what you should have achieved.

It is important to have a rough idea of the value of your property before inviting any agents over, so that you can identify when an agent is being unrealistic like this. If a property is on the market for much more than it's worth, then it's unlikely to get many enquiries. When properties are priced accurately, this generates more enquiries and more viewings, which gives the agent a better chance of negotiating the best possible price for you. A competitive market may even push you over your asking price! To get an idea of the true value, you can research sold prices in your area on sites like Zoopla. These figures are far more indicative of the true value than other asking values. You can ignore Zoopla's generated estimates though, as these are about as accurate as my estimate of 100 being the highest number.

Ideally, you also want to avoid instructing multiple agents. Not only will this end up costing you, in most cases, double the fees, but if your property is online with three or so different agents, it's not a good look. Buyers are psychologically put off by this. You would like to think that, by having multiple agents marketing your property, they will be able to work together to achieve the best result for you, their client. But this is usually very far from what happens, as they tend to start working against each other, to the detriment of your sale. You will get more organic enquiries by instructing one agent who you trust to put their all into it.

The final, and arguably the most important thing to consider when choosing your agent is: do you like them? Did you get on well with the agent? Did you find them overly pushy or salesy? Think about their likeability factor, because this is the person that will be meeting prospective buyers to show your house to, and if you didn't like them, then do you really trust them with this privilege? If you get along well with them then so will your potential buyers. To put this to the test, you can 'mystery shop' the various agents you're considering. Give them a call as a buyer and see how they deal with the enquiry. Did they follow you up after speaking/meeting with you? These are good indicators of a good or bad agent.

If you want to make your house easy to sell, make it easy to buy

- Anonymous

- **(AMBER) Bins** – Rubbish and recycling bins at the front of a property can be very unattractive, especially in the UK where we get a lot of wind which can blow them all over the place. Try to put your bins out of sight, somewhere down a side passage, tucked away in your back garden, or tight against a wall in your front garden. The ideal approach would be to get some kind of cover for them, so you can keep them at the front without being blatantly visible. There are also little containers you can get, that look like small bike sheds, which are for storing bins.

If you can't put them out of sight, just make sure they're as tidy as possible. Across the UK, we have up to 600,000 foxes during spring/summer (their peak mating season) ravaging through our bins, so it's important when marketing your property to make sure the exterior is always tidy, and the street isn't covered in your old newspapers and banana skins.

I've hosted many viewings where the bins have blown on to the pathway, blocking entry to the property, or where bins have tipped over. Whether it be down to the foxes or the Great British wind, the exterior of your property is the first impression viewers will have, so it's essential you don't let something as simple as bins hold you back at the first hurdle.

- **(AMBER) Bedrooms** – The bedroom is a sacred room. It's where you finally get to rest at the end of a long day, it's where kids can escape from their annoying younger sibling, and it's just everyone's safe space, hence it's important to have your bedrooms looking at their best when you're preparing your property for viewings.

So what do you need to focus on? The end goal is to make the room feel both cosy, and spacious; somewhere viewers can picture as their

safe haven, but also not feel trapped or cramped. Make sure you clear all the clutter. This means the floor is completely free of anything that doesn't belong there. Keep your beds and wardrobes, you can even keep your armchair if you have one in there, but put away any clothes, toys, books, and any loose items, with the end goal of maximising the floor space. If you have a chair you can easily move, I'd probably take that out as well, just to give the impression that the room is as big as you can possibly make it feel. Make your dressing tables and bedside tables look tidy, ideally putting away your makeup, hairbrushes, and anything else you might have there, but if this isn't possible, and you have nowhere to store these items, then buy a little basket to hold everything in one place. Just make it as tidy as you can.

You'll also want to make the room as bright as possible, which I know can be difficult in some cases, but all you need to do is maximise the light coming into the bedroom from an external source, aka Mr Sunshine. Completely open up any curtains or blinds you have, and let that light in. It's best to avoid having to turn lights on for daytime viewings, because this tends to give viewers the impression that the room is just dark, so do everything you can to avoid this when prepping for viewings.

The final note for bedrooms is to make your beds. You won't believe the amount of times I've walked into a bedroom on a viewing to be greeted by the beautiful sight of dirty boxer shorts, on a creased pillow, with a stained duvet hanging off the bed. In an ideal world, you'd make your beds to hotel standard, but I know this isn't always realistic, so you can just fluff your pillows, cover the bed with your duvet, try to tuck it in as tight as you can to avoid creases, and if you have a blanket then fold that neatly over the duvet. If possible, use white/bright covers because this helps to present the room in a brighter manner and can make the room appear larger. Plain covers are best, so pack up your Winnie the Pooh sheets and save them for your new home. A throw and a couple of cushions are a great, inexpensive addition, and can give your bedroom the hotel touch. I often advise buyers to flick through some of the holiday rental advertisements on websites like Airbnb because these places are selling the dream. If you look carefully, the rooms are often nothing special, however the scatter cushions, and tightly tucked duvet/throw, transport buyers to pampering hotel heaven.

◑ **Bathroom (RED/GREEN)** – A bathroom has the ability to add up to 5% to your property's value, but see 'I' for 'Investment' before jumping in and spending a small fortune. There is no doubt that a 'Wow' bathroom can be a selling point but in some cases, a small spruce can be enough.

● **(RED)** Some improvements won't cost you a penny. Just like a bedroom, it's important to declutter and clean your bathroom – but more so! Do not leave shower gel caps or razors lying around, clean up any shaving foam stains or toothpaste splatters, splash a bit of bleach down the loo, and check for hair everywhere. Other people's hair is just nasty and very off putting! If you want someone to imagine lying in your bath and sitting on your loo, they need to be able to take that leap of faith without the thought of a stray hair floating in their bubble bath. Do not leave ANYTHING out! The only exception is your chance to display the beautiful soaps and room candles that you have been saving for best. This room is all about pamper. I have worked extensively in serviced accommodation and holiday lettings, and we always know that this is one of the most important rooms for removing any trace of a former user. You should also leave a couple of neatly folded, fluffy, clean towels out to help with the aesthetic of the room.

○ **(GREEN)** One of the more simple adjustments you can make, is removing carpets from the bathroom. Carpets in bathrooms are an old fashioned quirk, from a different generation. I have never taken a buyer for a viewing at one of these properties who didn't immediately talk about ripping up the carpet. It won't cost you too much, but it will really help with your sale if you put down some inexpensive lino or, better still, tile the bathroom. The same here goes for dated decor, with yellow, green, and believe it or not I've even seen bright orange coloured tiles. You're better off with a bright, white bathroom – it's a neutral tone that makes the room feel bright and makes buyers a lot happier.

Another relatively inexpensive job is to join up rooms if you have your toilet in a separate room to the bath/shower. Buyers generally like larger rooms, and the joined loo/bathroom is considered more contemporary. Some buyers just don't want to do any work and are less likely to buy a house with the separate layout. Most are separated by a simple stud wall that is usually relatively cheap to remove. If at all possible, have it removed so that you are not forced to reflect the work in the price of the property down the line.

Just like the bedroom, the bathroom is a very important room because this is where you look after yourself and become vulnerable. You'll be hard pressed to find someone who feels content bathing in a thirty year-old, rusty bath with a sink that has forty year-old stains on. This is why a slick bathroom can make all the difference. Most buyers will favour a white suite, and you can pick up a three-piece suite very cheaply to make it look like a million dollars, with fancy taps. It really doesn't have to cost a fortune, but it could cost you dearly if this room is neglected.

It can also help to have both a bath and a shower. Lots of properties only have a shower, and many only have room for a shower, which is fair enough, but if you have the space to do so then get a bath. One of my old clients had a 1500 square foot house which didn't have a single bath in the entire property, and instead had a seven foot long shower in their family bathroom. Why? Because they're "not bath people". I appreciate that, but when you're going to sell your house it can be a dealbreaker for prospective buyers, so it's definitely worth filling that seven foot space with a bath. It will automatically increase your chances of achieving a quick sale at a good price. Families, in particular, will often discard houses without baths.

Further to considering putting in a bath, you should also consider putting in a downstairs toilet if you don't have one. People, especially families, like having more than one toilet, particularly having one downstairs, and this can be a real deal breaker. I've sold various properties without one, and on each occasion this was our biggest objection from buyers.

These suggestions are things that you will need to spend some money on, but it's better to look at them as an investment, not a cost. In making these amendments the value and saleability of your property increases, so this will more than make up for the temporary void in your bank account. A like for like refurb, with plain white tiles and a plain white bathroom suite, can be very inexpensive, it may well add to your sales value and, most importantly, it could be the difference between a buyer choosing your home over a similar one up the road.

● **(RED) Board** – I would always advise putting up a 'For Sale' board, prominently displayed outside your property. This lets all passing traffic – by foot, bike, or motor vehicle – know that your home is available to buy. Some people don't want their neighbours knowing they're selling, and others feel that putting a board up is just inviting other agents to knock on their door and bombard them with phone calls, but believe me, with or without a board, anyone nosy enough (especially other agents) can find out that your house is for sale using the internet.

I would say, in my experience, that close to a fifth of our enquiries came from random people who just happened to pass by one of our boards, so the pros far outweigh the cons and, by not having a board,, you could be missing out on a large pool of prospective buyers. You want to have the biggest possible marketing reach to maximise your chances of a strong sale, so don't miss out by refusing a board. You only need one buyer to make the right offer for your one property. Don't miss out if that one buyer walks by your house and offers on the house with a board just up the road.

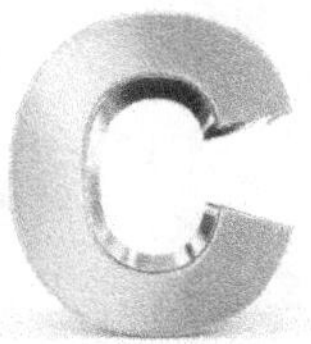

● **(AMBER) Clean windows** – In 'B' we spoke a lot about bright rooms being a big selling point. If your windows are covered in dirt or any sort of grime, it doesn't make the property seem loved or looked after. Cleaning your windows will help with the outside appearance of the property but it will also allow more light to come inside. It's a subtle thing but it certainly makes a difference.

○ **(GREEN) Carpets** – Similarly to bathrooms with their sometimes bright, dated decor, carpets can have a pretty dramatic effect on any room of the house. If you have an old, worn out, stained carpet, this is going to be a natural deterrent for buyers. Carpets can also carry years of lingering smells, for example if you are a smoker or if a smoker has previously lived in your house, then this smell will have settled into the carpets and will bless the whole room/property with the aroma. It is worth tearing out the carpets in this case, and either investing in polished floorboards/laminate, or in buying a new carpet. As a rule, carpet is most desirable in bedrooms, and laminate or real wood flooring in living areas. If you do not want to invest in new floor coverings, then the minimum you should consider with old carpets is to pay a professional company to come and deep clean. The difference can be astonishing and the return on investment is considerable.

Plan your work for today, and every day, then work your plan

- Margaret Thatcher

● **(RED) Declutter** – This is something we've already touched on quite a lot, in terms of decluttering your bedroom/bathroom, but this applies for the entire property. If you have lots of toys, niknaks, and just general, unnecessary stuff that doesn't really need to be out, then find somewhere to store it. Not only is this good as a temporary measure for viewings to make the property feel bigger, but when moving you should use the opportunity to get rid of some of your clutter anyway. This will take away a lot of stress during your move, and a decluttered home leads to a healthier mind. Garage sales, and sticking unwanted items on eBay or Facebook groups, are great ways to declutter, but you can also consider renting an external storage space if you run out of room in your own property.

○ **(GREEN) Decor** – Again, this has been touched on when talking about the decor of your bathrooms and carpets, but this is apparent throughout the house. The colour of your walls, the layout of your furniture, and the overall condition of the decoration of your property, can all cause a potential buyer to either love or hate it instantly. You'd hope that buyers can inject some imagination in terms of what they're going to do to put their own stamp on the property, but a lot of the time they can't see past what's there. Of course, it's my job as an agent to paint the picture for them, but you'll also find a lot of buyers would like to be able to move in and live there for a while before doing any work, and if the decor isn't up to scratch then they won't see this as a possibility.

First things first, cure any mould or damp spots. This is the single biggest objection I've experienced from buyers. If a property has the slightest hint of damp, the buyer will either discard the property because of the implications of damp, or they'll drag their feet getting a damp survey done, which can quite easily lead to a fallthrough. What you can do as the seller, in order to avoid this, is to get a damp survey done yourself. They are usually free of charge, and give you a good idea of a) how much of a damp problem there actually is, and b) how much it'll cost to fix. At this point, you can either pay to fix it yourself, pre-sale, or you can provide the report to your agent who can relay it on to prospective buyers. If you don't want to, or can't afford to, fix the issue yourself, then providing the report goes a long way towards putting a buyer's mind at ease because they know how much it will cost to sort it out themselves, giving them a sense of certainty that it can be resolved. Damp is one of the biggest ways that people try to get a reduction on price, so it's worth addressing the issue beforehand if you can. Unfortunately, decorating over the damp spot is not an option. It doesn't cure the root of the problem, and if you do this the damp will just quickly reappear through the paint/wallpaper.

Otherwise, with decor, you need to be looking at the colour of your walls. Are they a neutral tone, or do you have bright, coral-themed wallpaper? Some buyers may have the same taste as you and appreciate the quirky wallpaper, but most of them will just see it as another cost for them to remove it. The same goes for peeling wallpaper. Over time, your wallpaper may naturally start peeling off due to age, so either replace it, or stick it back on – a super easy and cheap fix that will make a huge difference.

The end goal with decor is to have your property looking as bright, neutral, and up-to-date as possible, because you really want to limit the amount of money a buyer feels they need to spend upon making the purchase.

● **(RED) Empty bins** – From rotten eggs to X-rated magazines, I've seen it all in my vendors' bins. We all know the grotesque smell that bins produce when they've been full for too long, so put yourself in the position of a viewer. If you're looking around a property, and you smell that pungent odour, you don't necessarily know where it's coming from or what's caused it, but it leaves a negative anchor in your mind about that property. It also suggests that the owner doesn't really look after their property, so it is essential your bins are not smelly and are not too full when preparing your house for viewings. It could even be worth using some air freshener before viewings in order to put a positive association into the prospective buyer's mind.

You can't use up creativity. The more you use, the more you have

- Maya Angelou

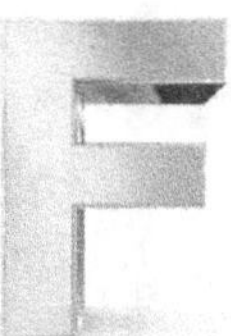

● **(RED) First impressions** – We've already briefly covered this, when talking about those pesky bins at the front of your house, but first impressions really are everything. Studies have shown that it takes buyers eight minutes to decide whether they like a property or not, while 60% of purchasers will rule a property out before they even walk through the front door, feeling trepidation within an average of four and a half minutes.

With this in mind, there are a couple of things to consider, the first being that you choose an agent whom you can trust to be punctual. I have met buyers who have shown up at a property, for a viewing, where the agent was running late, giving them a good chance to get a feel for the area and the exterior before the viewing. As a result, they have been put off by something that they saw on the street, or by some aspect of the exterior of the house, so much so that they didn't end up even looking inside the property, cancelling the viewing instead. Your agent being punctual alleviates this issue more often than not, as they will get the buyers inside the house within those essential first few minutes, meaning that they get a full picture of what is on offer beyond the first impression of the facade.

More importantly, take a good, objective look at your curbside appeal. Try to see your home as a potential buyer will. Is the brickwork or paintwork chipped? Is your front garden overgrown? Are the bins messily on show? These are all issues you should look into fixing because not only are they the first things your viewers will see, they are also the last thing, so you want them to leave with a positive image of the property.

● **(AMBER) Facebook** – We are in an age where social and digital media have taken over. The social media advertising market is projected to reach $100 billion in 2020, a rise of 8.7 % on the previous year. Over 44 million people use Facebook in the UK alone, with over 2.6 billion active users worldwide as of 2020.... So where do you think is a good idea to market your property?

As discussed under the 'Agent' chapter, most high street agents will take your property, stick it on Rightmove and/or Zoopla, and let it sit there, waiting for enquiries to come through. They're missing out on this enormous market and huge pool of buyers. On the property portals, you get people browsing to see what's on the market, and you get people actively looking to buy. An advert on Facebook could fall into someone's feed who had no initial plans on moving, but they see this beautifully marketed property, and suddenly their interest is sparked. With Facebook ads you'll also reach potential buyers from other countries, including, but definitely not limited to, foreign investors.

This is the way estate agency is moving, with more and more of the cutting edge, self-employed agents moving their business in this direction and getting a large number of their sales from Facebook advertising campaigns. Not all properties are suited to Facebook campaigns, and some agents will charge a small premium for this marketing, but it can be well worth the investment.

○ **(GREEN) Flowers** – Flowers can really lift a room and give that 'feel good' factor. The smell, the colourful, bright look. Having plants inside a property is well known to improve mental health, and it really helps with the overall aesthetic of a property too. If you don't want to look after/buy fresh flowers, you can buy some very good fake ones. It may just be my ignorance, but I can rarely tell the difference between real and fake until I smell them!

● **(RED) Floorplans** – I see so many agents advertising without a floorplan, and I just don't get it. Having a floorplan helps buyers visualise the property better when they're looking at listings online, and also helps during/after viewings, as most buyers will have some sort of an idea of the rough measurements of their furniture, so they can start thinking about what kind of layout they'll have, and if their furniture will fit. A lot of the time, people choose to view a property based on the floorplans alone, because size and layout matter. If you don't have floorplans, you're far more likely to be scrolled past.

It's tangible, it's solid, it's beautiful it's artistic, from my standpoint, and I just love real estate

- Donald Trump

● **(RED) Garden or outside space** – Outside spaces became highly desirable in 2020 in the post-Coronavirus lockdown era. Whilst everyone was cooped up at home for months, meaning they were only able to leave the house once per day to exercise, that little slice of outdoor paradise became an absolute must for many. Some people were lucky enough to own a garden or balcony, while many others did not have this luxury, so once the property market reopened, outside space was at the top of most buyer's lists.

Have you ever been browsing on the property portals and come across the most beautiful garden? You see it and it immediately catches your eye. Well, if you're selling a property with a garden, your aim should be to make yours just as eye catching … and it's easily done. You want to make it look like an attractive space where people will want to spend time. If your garden is muddy and overgrown, this is very off putting. Many people view a garden/balcony as an extra room, or an extension of the house, so it really can be a dealbreaker. I've always said that a house with a beautifully presented garden, or a well kept balcony, can almost sell itself, no matter what the interior looks like.

If you don't have a lawn, or it's patchy, then plant some grass seed. It's so easy to grow in just a couple of weeks! Once you have a full lawn, maintain and cut it. Long, messy grass can make a garden look unsightly. A quick mow can have it looking neat, making all the difference, even without flowers and other decorative plants. You should also cut back overhanging trees and overgrown bushes. Not only can these look unattractive from the outside, they can also block light from getting inside the property, and make your garden appear to be smaller than it is. It may be worth investing in a few colourful planted pots or hanging baskets, which garden centres sell for £10-20. They can make the garden more enticing, and can move with you to your new home once you have achieved the best price for your current home.

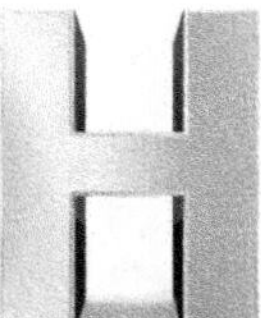

○ **(GREEN) Hobnob** – Hobnobbing, believe it or not, is a verb which means to mix socially. By talking to your neighbours, they can recommend any good agents that they might have previously used, and they may even know someone who is looking to buy in your area, so let them know when you put your home on the market. You can also benefit from their home improvement recommendations, any local contacts they have to carry out these home improvements, and you never know, they may even be interested in buying your house themselves!

● **(RED) Hotel finish** – Make your whole house look like a hotel, with perfectly made beds, fluffy towels, zero clutter. You really want to be selling the dream, enabling buyers to picture themselves sipping a cup of tea in the kitchen, reading their newspaper in bed, and sitting by the toasty fireplace in the winter.

Plans are nothing; planning is everything

- Dwight D. Eisenhower

● **(AMBER) Say goodbye to the I** – You need to depersonalise your home. You may be so proud of your Thai elephant collection, or the photos of your grandchildren, but buyers need to be able to imagine their own 'I' in your property. This doesn't mean to say that you should take *everything* down, because it's also nice for buyers to feel that your house has been loved and lived in by a warm, happy person/family. They can also picture their artwork or family pictures up in the spaces where you have yours. It is just a general rule that neutral is best and this includes personal possessions. People HAVE to be able to imagine this as THEIR home. Make this as easy for them as possible by removing everything that shouts YOU.

● **(AMBER) Investment** – Does your home have investment appeal? Could someone turn it into apartments? A rental property? A property twice the size? Could it be rented out for Airbnb or holiday lettings? We've talked a lot about doing various bits of renovation to your property, but this does not account for investors who come in actively looking for a big project, something they can add value to. As an agent, I've always had a long list of cash buyers, developers, and people who relish the opportunity to do a project, so when choosing your agent, make sure they know the investment side of things, and are able to talk to investors about how every bit of value could be added to your property.

A large part of an agent's job is painting a picture for buyers, so that they can see themselves living in a property, and the same goes for developers who may need some pointers on what a finished product could look like. Has anyone developed a house like yours locally? Examples are great to have, as they give a good idea of what is possible with the local planning department, and you may even have a pre-planning report made up with your local planning department. This is much cheaper than a full planning application but will give any developer some reassurance as to what might be possible. With this in mind, it is a good idea to choose an agent who has experience with developers. Even better, some agents also have experience as a developer themselves. These agents know what a developer is looking for in a property, and can sell to other developers a lot more capably. They can also match property and builders to potential investors. Be careful of over-promising, though. Estate Agents slip 'STPP' into their details for good reason. STPP (Subject To Planning Permission) means 'Buyer beware'. You can't offer the chance to build a three story extension unless you either have full planning permission, or remind the buyer that this would be STPP.

O **(GREEN) Incentive** – This is not something that you see happening a lot in resale property, it is more in the domain of new builds, but it can make a huge difference if you are willing or able to offer some sort of an incentive to prospective buyers. This is something that I would not necessarily advise, unless you have been struggling to sell, and any incentive scheme will need discussion with a legal professional before being offered.

Stamp duty is a big cost that clobbers buyers' budgets nationwide. First time buyers get free stamp duty up to £300,000, saving them £5,000, and for properties up to £500,000, they pay no stamp duty on the first £300,000. As a result of this, you find many first time buyers not wanting to exceed a £300,000 budget, with some willing to go up to £500,000 but no higher. In my experience, I've worked with a lot of first time buyers with big dreams to own a gorgeous, humongous house, but in most parts of London £500,000 isn't going to get you that, which leaves them disappointed, with a dilemma. A nice incentive, with this in mind, is to offer to pay their stamp duty for them. In doing this, you can factor your extra cost into the price, so the buyer doesn't have to find the cash to pay the stamp duty themselves, and instead can use their mortgage to cover that additional cost.

You can also consider offering to pay their solicitor's fees. This is a significantly cheaper option than paying their stamp duty, but it still goes a long way and is a nice gesture. I've been finding more and more sellers offering this incentive more recently.

● **(RED) Joshua Glanville** – Instruct Joshua Glanville to sell your house.... This one goes without saying.

○ **(GREEN) Juliet balcony** - Juliet balconies are narrow balconies or railings, which sit just outside doors on upper floors of a property. They were made famous by the star-crossed lovers Romeo and Juliet, with Juliet reciting the famous line "Romeo, Romeo, wherefore art thou Romeo?" on one of these balconies. They are fairly quick and easy to install, and often do not require planning permission (but please check!). You will not gain more floor space from installing one, but it will increase the amount of light coming into a room, as they are normally complemented by big glass doors, and can give the feeling of being on a balcony when you are actually still sitting or standing inside your property. Whether or not you would consider this a form of outside space, it is still an attractive prospect for buyers.

**Who ever loved that loved not at first sight
(first impressions)**

\- Christopher Marlowe

● **(RED) Kerb appeal** – This can be everything. As already discussed, people have often made a decision about whether or not they are interested in buying a property just from how it looks on the outside before they step over the threshold. This means it's important that you get the property looking its best on the outside – not just on the inside.

◑ **(GREEN/RED) Kitchen** – A good kitchen can add up to 10% on to a property's value, but is a very individual choice. Some people prefer a big, bright kitchen, with a breakfast bar backing on to their garden, with bifolding doors, while others prefer something cosier and more basic. Just like with bathrooms, but arguably more so, on viewings, installing a kitchen is one of the biggest adjustments people talk about making.

○ **(GREEN)** A property's kitchen is one of its biggest sellers. If your kitchen is outdated or shabby, not chic, then I would not necessarily recommend installing a whole new kitchen (although, as stated above, this can add a lot of value), because buyers tend to have varying tastes when it comes to kitchens so there is a chance they will just rip it out anyway. Regardless, if you don't want to spend a larger sum of money on a new kitchen, then there are some smaller, less costly, things you can do to improve how it looks, without breaking the bank.

Replace worktops. Putting a new worktop on a kitchen can instantly make it feel fresh again, especially if your worktops are dated, stained or chipped at all.

Paint or replace cupboard doors. If the cupboards are dated, but the carcasses are still functional and sturdy, then you could paint them to make it feel like a new kitchen. If the doors are not standard size, then there are now plenty of companies that custom make cupboard doors, at a reasonable price, if you want to replace them, which I would recommend doing if they are damaged, off the hinge, or dated. Simply doing this can completely change the way your kitchen looks and make it feel new.

Replace tiles. The tiles in a kitchen can often date a property, so it could be a good idea to replace them with something more modern or neutral, to bring the kitchen more up-to-date and have a wider appeal.

● **(RED)** As with every other room when preparing for viewings, declutter! Don't have your surfaces full of empty milk cartons, crumbs or smeared surfaces. Clear the table, and tidy the cupboards, because it is likely that viewers will open up the cupboards to see what kind of space there is.

One tip I give sellers is, when you have a last minute viewing, grab a carrier bag and put all bits and bobs, bills and phone chargers etc. in the bag, and then hide it in the washing machine. Just get the clutter out of the way. I have had buyers discover the secret stash, on occasion, while inspecting inside the washing machine (yes, they do this sometimes!) but it has only ever raised a smile.

● **(RED) Light** – I have been to so many properties where I've been so shocked by how dark the owner has left it, that I've learnt to show up to viewings early purely to make sure there is sufficient light, and if there isn't, then to open up some blinds and curtains and do everything I can to let the light come in. Sunlight triggers our brains to release endorphins that make us happy. In Australia I've always been amazed at how happy and content everyone seems to be, and I do believe that a large factor in this is the fact that they have blazing sun for large parts of the year. In the UK, we don't get anywhere near as much sun, so we've got to make the most of what we do get. Buyers will always be turned on by a property which has lots of natural light coming through.... Properties online which have bright photos generate far more enquiries for a reason!

In the winter months, we get very little sunlight here in the UK, which can make this part difficult. To counteract this, we need to make sure that all of your lights are turned on ready for viewings. Furthermore, if you have an outside light, turn it on, and leave it on, until you go to bed, so that people passing by can see your home. During the daytime, open up all of your curtains/blinds fully, try to remove shrubbery or anything close to your windows, and turn on any lamps you have. Lamps can make dark corners look brighter but can also help to make a property feel cozy. You could also light a fire in the colder months to make the house feel cozier and more homely.

The end goal here is to have as much natural light as possible, minimising the use of electric lights, but I know this cannot always be done so we have to adjust as and when appropriate. At the end of the day, as long as there's no dark rooms, that's the most important thing.

● **(AMBER) Lay the table for dinner** – Put out your best plates, glasses, napkins and cutlery, as if it is a restaurant. This helps people to imagine themselves in your home, entertaining for their friends and family. A bowl of fruit or some wrapped bonbons can be enticing too.

● **(RED) Leaflets** – A good agent will canvass the streets around you, letting them know that your house is on the market. They should get your permission to do so first, and I would always advise accepting this proposal. How this can benefit you is that there will be plenty of people renting in the area, who may be thinking of buying. If they like your area, and see a new house on the market there, they could be interested. Furthermore, people may be living in a smaller property in the area and may want to upsize, or they may want to be closer to a certain part of town. You never know what could come up from this canvassing exercise.

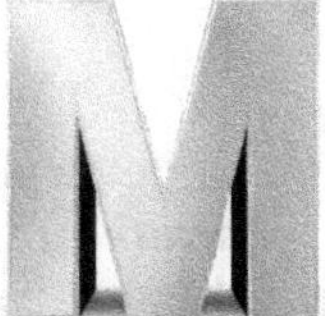

● **(RED) Mail** – Remove your mail from the doormat before viewings. A large pile of mail left on the floor can make it hard for viewers to even get through the door, and it can also make the property feel unwelcoming or neglected. I have one particular viewing horror story, from when I visited a property which had laminate flooring in the hallway. We walked into the property, and there was a great big pile of post on the floor. I let the viewer walk ahead whilst I closed the door and went to pick up the post, which was my big mistake as he trod on a stray envelope and slipped, falling backwards in a cartoonesque banana skin manner and banging his backside. This is never going to be an ideal start to a viewing, and I am happy to confess he didn't buy the house. When arriving at a viewing early, picking up the post is now one of the first things I do in order to avoid this from happening again, so try and make this part of your agent's job easier!

● **(RED) Marketing** – You could have an incredible property, in a desirable location, but if it's not being marketed well then you will never sell it. We've already covered this in depth, but just to reiterate my message, high street agents market in a very passive way. They will list your property on their website, Rightmove and Zoopla, with some photos, a floorplan and a brief description on their website, then sit and wait for the enquiries to come in, maybe calling through their database if they're in the mood that day. This is why it can take them months to sell a property! The best agents will do all of the above, but also push a property all over social media, and various other platforms, coming up with an in-depth plan with the seller on the best approach to sell their property for the best price, as quickly as possible, ensuring everyone who could possibly be aware of the property is, in fact, aware of the property. Getting your marketing right is essential and this begins with choosing the right agent.

● **(RED) Neighbourhood** – Depending on where you live, a lot of your prospective buyers will be moving from another area. It is important that you choose an agent who really knows your area, including things such as the best local restaurants, shops, schools, closest stations, local events etc.… Having said this, every street can be different, with local events, community groups and street parties varying from street to street, so let your agent know of anything that might be worth knowing. Anything that can contribute to a buyer feeling that this is going to be the right area for them is worth mentioning. What's amazing about your area? Go above and beyond and write a list of things that make your area special, which can be handed to your buyers on viewings!

66

I like an interior that defies labelling. I don't really want someone to walk into a room and know that I did it

- Bunny Williams

● **(RED) Open house** – Like quite a few of the concepts we've discussed in this book, an 'open house' is generally perceived as quite an Americanised approach to selling a house. Over in the US, they hold open house after open house until they find a buyer, and this works with great success. I remember there was one property I wanted to view out in Fort Lauderdale, South Florida, which had a board outside, with a great big image of the realtor's face on, accompanied by an 'Open House' slip underneath it. I pulled up at the property and knocked on the door, but unfortunately the open house slot had just ended. The agent told me they were doing TWO open houses PER DAY at the property until it was sold, so I could come back tomorrow. The closest thing British high street agents have to this is called a 'block viewing', where they organise to have people view a property in back to back timeslots, usually once per week, but only for the properties they deem the most saleable.

Both of these approaches create a sense of urgency with buyers, as it means that they see other people looking around, potentially showing an interest in the property, and it's simply in our nature to fear the possibility of missing out (more commonly known these days as FOMO). If someone else wants what you're looking at, even if you are not particularly interested at that point, you will suddenly become a lot more interested – it triggers urgency. With the 'block viewing' approach, the viewers *may* see each other in passing, whereas with an 'open house' this is guaranteed, with possible interactions even occurring between the viewers. Open houses are becoming more popular in the UK amongst the more innovative agents, and typically result in an offer (or two) being made for your property on the same day. This is a great way to launch a new property to the market.

● **(AMBER) Original use** – Putting your rooms back to their original use is helpful. Some people don't need that second or third bedroom, so they turn it into a study or a gym room. Try to put these back to the use they were originally intended for. Buyers can sometimes find it hard imagining a house with that extra room if they can only see what is there in that moment. In the area I mostly covered as a high street agent, a typical house would have three sizable double bedrooms, and a fourth, much smaller bedroom. A lot of the time the owners would turn the smallest bedroom into an office, just sticking a desk, chair and maybe a bookshelf in there. This created many objections, as lots of buyers just couldn't see past what was there, arguing that you couldn't even fit a bed in there. This issue was very easily resolved every time by advising the seller to take their desk out and replace it with a bed, just while we are marketing the property, and suddenly buyers were able to see that this is, in fact, a bedroom which you CAN fit a full sized bed in!

○ **(GREEN) Privacy** – An overlooked garden is a big turn off for buyers, so consider putting up fencing or hedging, if it will help to prevent this. In some instances this is not possible, especially if you live in an urban or congested suburban area, but it's a good idea to do the best you can, to make it feel as private as possible. One of my previous vendors went a bit over the top with this, by getting a landscape gardener to design a garden for her, which had tall trees hanging over the top, so that she wouldn't be overlooked by the block of flats parallel to the back of her house. I wouldn't recommend taking it to this extreme, as it was constantly dark and cold there!

If you are in a ground floor apartment, with communal gardens, check your lease to see if the area around your access point is part of your title, and what you are allowed to do with it. My first property had a huge communal garden. The previous owner had failed to notice that a large area surrounding my apartment was actually designated in the title for my private use. I cordoned this off, put in some beautiful decking and patio furniture, and voila, I suddenly had a private garden AND communal garden. This added substantial value to the property.

○ **(GREEN) Paint** – It's okay, we all have our own taste, even you with the bright green walls! But people can really be put off by these extravagant, bright colours in a property, and the same goes for darker colours, which can make a room feel smaller. The same vendor mentioned above (with the over-sized trees) had her back room painted a dark green, while her front room was painted a bright yellow colour, so you'd be overwhelmed by the front room, then walk into this polar opposite, dark back room with a gloomy, shaded garden. It was a tough sale!

Instead of bright colours, opt for more neutral colours, and, if you want to add personality or colour to a room, then do it through accessories such as cushions, flowers, paintings etc. On the other hand, this is rarely a deal breaker, as repainting a room is one of the more minor refurbishments a buyer can carry out themselves, just remember that not all buyers want to do the work, and not all buyers have the imagination to see a property with a neutral colour scheme. If you can give them a hand on this, and it won't break the bank to do so, then why not!

You should also consider touching up your paintwork. Over time, our walls, doors, skirting boards, and even ceilings inevitably suffer wear and tear. Touching up the paintwork, or even giving them a fresh coat of paint, can have a big effect on the room. If your paint has become thin, or chipped, it makes the property feel older and less loved.

● **(RED) Photos** – This one is essential, as the photos of your property can either make or break your listing. Well taken, bright photos online can help to attract more enquiries, meaning more people through the door for viewings, hence increasing your chance of a sale at the best price. Most estate agents now photoshop their photos to make them look as clean and bright as possible, however if you are not happy with the photos they take, then you should ask them to take them again, or alternatively supply your own.

The sweet spot for photos on your online listing is around 8-10. Any more than this, and buyers start to get a bit bored of scrolling, and start to feel they've got a good idea of what the property is really like. If you limit the number of photos on the listing, simply uploading the best pictures of your best rooms, this will leave the buyers wanting more, increasing the chances of viewings being booked in. By limiting the number of photos, this also means you can update/rotate the photos if one set of photos isn't generating results. If your property has been on the market for a while, then get some new photos taken, or switch up the ones you have to keep your listing fresh-looking. If you have a garden, get some new photos of it taken when the sun is out and all the flowers are in bloom. Get rid of any photos with things such as Christmas trees in them, if it's no longer seasonally appropriate. Having a picture of a Christmas tree in June makes the listing feel ancient!

Don't be afraid to ask your agent to digitally enhance your photos. It's now so easy to adjust light and colour levels to make a room look brighter.

○ **(GREEN) Planning permission** – If there is the potential to do some major works to your property, such as an extension or a loft conversion, then it can add value to apply for planning permission in advance of your sale. This is particularly relevant if you are likely to sell to developers. This does not mean you are going to do the work/pay for the work yourself, it just means that you sell the house WITH planning permission for said work, which makes the prospect more attractive to buyers who can also add some value on to the house. If you've always thought about adding an extension to the property, but have never been able to afford it, or you've just not got around to it, by securing this planning permission, you can show buyers the potential of the property, and give them peace of mind that the permission is already in place before they put in an offer. A cheaper alternative is to obtain pre-planning permission, which is not binding, but gives a good indication as to what works might be permitted by the council planning department.

If you have had works done yourself, then make sure you have your planning permission documents and building control certificates to hand, ready for conveyancing. If you have had work done without permission as it fell under permitted development then it is worth applying for a certificate of lawful development from the council. If you have had any new windows, then search out your FENSA certificates; any electrical or gas work or new boilers? Fish out your compliance certificates. Any damp proofing work or woodworm treatments? Grab those guarantees. A lack of paperwork can cause delays, increasing the chances of a fallthrough and creating last minute reductions.

● **(RED) Permitted development** – Make sure your agent knows what can and can't be done under permitted development, for example knowing the regulated length/width of a potential extension or conversion before it needs full planning permission, and all the regulations surrounding any other work that can be done without obtaining legal authorisation first. Potential can add great value to a property and should be highlighted by the agent (STPP).

● **(RED) Quirks** – What 'quirks' does your property have? Does it have a hidden walk-in wardrobe, or an underground weapon room (this one is scarily more common than you'd like to think in the US)? Let your agent know, although bear in mind that not all conversation starters like this are selling points. Consider whether your property's quirks can be disguised or removed if they aren't truly selling points, and if they are desirable, then ensure your agent knows and plays on this, as any good salesperson would do.

See if you can turn an unattractive quirk to your advantage. A loo at the bottom of the garden is not a selling point, but the same brick-built outbuilding used as a small home office or kids' playhouse might be.

The only failure is not to try

- George Clooney

○ **(GREEN) Rendering** – If the outside of your property is pebble-dash, or an unattractively painted brick, then rendering a property can greatly transform its appearance and give it much greater kerb appeal. Some surfaces, such as fake stone cladding, or types of pebble-dash, are hugely unpopular, and as is poorly painted brick which you see a lot of in ex-local authority properties. Render is a very modern finish and can be a good investment. This is one of the bigger jobs that buyers never seem to be as willing to do, and as already discussed, this is the first impression they will have of the property, so it makes a big difference. Rendering also often comes with a weather-proofing guarantee, which offers an added bonus.

● **(RED) Resale value** – Put yourself in a buyer's shoes. If you were looking at your property, would you buy it? Something buyers tend to consider, especially developers, is how much potential there is to sell the property in the future. With ex-local authority properties, you are less likely to gain as much value over time as you would with any other property, and the same goes for properties in certain areas. This is something you need to consider when thinking about the valuation of your property, but of course there is not much you can do to change that side of things unless your property is a complete 'doer upper'. With local authority properties, I encourage sellers to really look at the curb-side appeal. If you can paint the exterior, or train a climbing rose over the front door, or add some tumbling window boxes, you can set yourself apart from the rest. Uniformity doesn't sell. What can you do to set your home apart?

● **(AMBER) Staging** – When a property developer has completed construction, and is trying to sell their property, they tend to furnish the property with sofas, tables, chairs, and some nice flowers to make it feel homely. I'm not saying that you should buy a new set of furniture, but just to stage your property so that it's tidy and feels warm and homely. This is a great way of getting someone to fall in love with it, and all goes back to our previous topics covering bed making, flowers, laying tables etc.…

If your property is empty, it is worth, at least, staging the living room and master bedroom. There are companies who rent furnishings for this purpose. Whether to do this or not is a discussion to be had with your agent, but it can certainly seal the deal on higher end properties.

● **(RED) Smell** – Something that also comes under the topic of staging is the smell of the property. No one likes the smell of wet dog, stale cigarettes, or strong, spicy cooking smells. Get some air freshener, spray some perfume, bake some bread or brew some coffee in the kitchen to help disguise the less attractive smells, and give it a homely, luxury feel. Burn some scented candles or essential oils in other rooms. Even sticking a potato in the oven smells yummy – just don't let it burn!

○ **(GREEN) Strip wooden doors and floors** – Stripping old wooden doors and floors can give them a new lease of life and give your property a unique appeal. Although this can take time, it can be worth it, looking particularly effective in period properties. It is often a cheaper alternative to new wooden flooring, and is especially popular with older properties.

● **(RED) Social media** – We've already talked about the importance of marketing using social media, namely Facebook, but there

are a plethora of other sites which can attract buyers. Twitter, Instagram, TikTok and, especially, Pinterest are phenomenal marketing tools to reach buyers who, otherwise, might not have otherwise come across your property. Lots of people want to purchase a property, and whilst they spend hours on social media, they are not inclined to sit, coming up with a search criteria on Rightmove, speaking with dozens of agents etc…. This approach reaches those people.

● **(RED) Schools** – This is a big one, and goes back to knowing your area and making sure your agent does too. What are the best local schools, and what school catchment areas are you inside of? In my experience, this is one of the biggest deal breakers considering there are always young families looking to move, and if you're not in the catchment area of a good school, this can rule out an entire category of buyer for you to focus your marketing on.

● **(RED) Tidy up** – This one goes back to decluttering, but I can't stress enough how important it is. We've covered many areas in this book which require expenditure of some sort, however this one just requires a few hours of your time. Timetable an hour a day until the clutter has gone. Make sure the property is clean, with no dust and no clutter, so it is looking as spick and span as possible. Prospective buyers won't appreciate having to step over your toddler's toys or looking at your dirty dishes from the night before! If it doesn't have a home that is out of sight then consider a short term storage unit until your sale is agreed. A messy house can cost you dearly.

● **(AMBER) Temperature** – Make sure the property's temperature is appropriately controlled. In the colder months, you want it to feel nice and snuggly. People really appreciate it (including me as the agent!) when they're standing in the freezing cold, then get to walk into a toasty property – it gives a positive and welcoming first impression. Let's face it, no one wants to live in a cold property (unless they're a vampire!). In the warmer months, which I know are scarce in the UK, keep your property cool. Open up your windows and doors to let a through breeze come in before viewings. Again, if someone has been standing, sweating in the sun before a viewing, it goes a long way for them to be able to step into a cool room. The ideal property is kept warm in the winter and cool in the summer, so show prospective buyers that yours can do this.

Success in real estate starts when you believe you are worthy of it

- Michael Ferrara

● **(RED) Underpants on the floor** – If you leave your dirty laundry on the floor, it's almost guaranteed you'll end up having an unscheduled viewing that day. Get into the habit of putting your clothes away, not leaving them on the back of a chair or on the floor. Again, the less clutter the better! You never know when buyers may want to show up, and you want to be in a position where you can accept as many viewings as you can, so keep your property tidy for as much of the time as you can. Many buyers won't give you a second chance, especially in a busy market where they will be viewing multiple properties in a short space of time.

**If you don't like where you are, then move.
You are not a tree**

- Jim Rohn

● **(AMBER) Video** – It is an unorthodox approach, which we are now seeing a lot more of due to the increase in the industry's need for technology following the Coronavirus pandemic. A video tour of your property is a great way to entice potential buyers, and gives a better idea of the layout and space available. Some estate agents, generally away from the high street, will now offer these. If they don't, and you think this could be a good marketing ploy, then ask if they would be willing/able to include a video on their listing. You can also share it on your social media and ask friends/family to do the same to increase your reach.

However, just like with photos, you don't want to give too much away in the video. You really want to sell the sizzle (the best parts of your property), and not the sausage (every single little detail). You want to leave the buyers wanting more, wanting to view the property to see these amazing features in person. The video should be bright, filmed well, and edited with the best possible angles.

● **(AMBER) Virtual walkthrough** – Technology these days is incredible. Not only can you take amazing photos and film a red hot video, but now there's also the option for 3D tours. These are made using special cameras that capture the entire 360 degree environment. Think of Google Maps' 'Street View' where you can choose any street in the world, and look around as if you're actually walking on the street…. You can now do this, but with your house! Not many agents in the UK offer this, but it is common in the US and is a real treat for prospective buyers, so just like with the video option, if this sounds good to you then ask your agent if it's a possibility.

If you can, you should, and if you're brave enough to start, you will

- Stephen King

○ **(GREEN) Window boxes** – Something that adds a huge amount of character to the facade of a house is window boxes. Generally filled with pretty flowers, they add colour and additional aesthetics which contribute towards buyers' first impression, and make the property look loved and cared for. If you have green fingers, then this is a lovely addition. If not, you can pick up some great fake plants in IKEA to fill up your window boxes. At window sill level, nobody will see the difference, and they last all year without watering!

○ **(GREEN) Wallpaper** – We've already talked about this under the 'Decor' topic, but it's worth reiterating. Some people love wallpaper, others hate it with a passion. If you have wallpaper in your property, try to look at it through fresh eyes. Does it have a bold, brightly coloured pattern on it which may not be liked by everyone? If so, it's probably worth replacing it, or painting over it, with something more neutral. If the wallpaper is peeling, then try to repair or replace it. This is another one of those things which isn't essential because it's fairly cheaply and easily done by a buyer, but it's worth thinking about.

○ **(GREEN) Windows** – If you have some rooms that are very dark, then adding windows can transform a dingy, closed space into something light and airy. You'll find a lot of bathrooms in particular which don't have a window installed, which is one of the more important rooms to have a window for, as you need to air it out to help avoid bad smells and damp. Building regulations stipulate that you should, at least, have a working fan in bathrooms, so if you don't have a window then make sure your bathroom fan is in good working order. One of my first memories working in property development was having to work with one of our builders to install a window. We turned a dark and

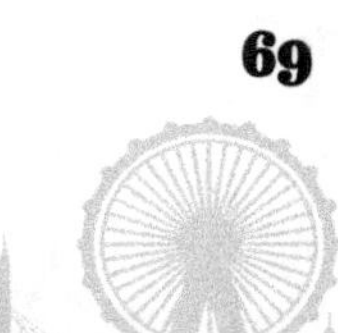

damp sauna room into a gorgeous, bright and sunny dining room. It was a great investment but, wow, I never realised how insanely heavy those things are before you install them!

Rooflights/skylights are also a nice feature to consider installing if your hallways are dark or your ceilings don't allow much light to come through. They always make the property a lot brighter and are generally picked up on by buyers as a nice selling point.

● **(RED) X-Ray** – This one is my favourite. You need to X-Ray your house! Of course, there is what buyers see on the surface, but the soul of a house is what determines its health when you put it on the market. When you're ready and have finished with all of your tweaks and preparations, ask a friend to come in and 'X-Ray' the house. What do they feel? Who do they see as your target market? Are there any changes they would make? Would THEY buy the house? If it doesn't fit with the kind of buyers you think you're after, then this approach can help you see that. Very often when we're looking at our own property, we see it through rose-tinted glasses because it's ours, and we love the features we've lived with over the years, but getting someone else in and asking for their honest opinion will help you see things you wouldn't necessarily have noticed before.

Generally, sellers see their properties as more valuable than they are, and buyers see properties as less valuable than they are. Get a friend over, and ask for an honest second opinion.

The most important quality for an investor is temperament, not intellect. You need a temperament that neither derives great pleasure from being with the crowd or against the crowd

- Warren Buffett

● **(RED) Yoyo agents** – We touched on this when talking about pricing your house and the kind of agents to avoid at all costs. Yoyo agents are the agents who start with a super high valuation/asking price, in order to entice sellers to list with them. This price then comes falling down with a thud as the buyers simply stay away, or come in with silly, super low offers. The agent then comes back to you after a short period of time requesting a price reduction. More thuds, and more price reductions later, and eventually the property either sells for way below what it should have achieved, or it becomes stale and remains at the lowest price level.

You are much better off finding a 'snowball agent'. Everyone loves that first snowball, piquing buyers' interest at the correct market value, and as the buyers come, then watch that snowball grow as the bidding begins.

○ **(GREEN) Yellow front doors** – Bold colours are very on trend at the moment. If you would like to stand out from the crowd, then why not improve your curbside appeal with one splash of colour on your front door. According to Country Living Magazine, bright yellow front doors feature in two of the top ten door colours. Purple and grey are also very popular at the moment.

For the record, I'm not saying this just because my favourite colour is yellow! When you're walking down a street with blue, white, red, fairly standard-coloured doors, which one is going to stand out to you? You'll remember the one with the bright yellow door, or even pink! That doesn't mean to say you should paint the interior or entire facade that colour as well – these colours are only meant for front doors!

Real estate provides the highest returns, the greatest values, and the least risk

- Armstrong Williams

● **(AMBER) Zoo** – Many people love cats, dogs, and yellow-bellied chameleons, but most people only love THEIR cats, dogs, and yellow-bellied chameleons. Your house isn't a zoo, so however gorgeous your pets are, see if you can leave as little trace as possible when buyers come. This means no smelly cat litter, hoover the cat fur/dog hair, no dog poo or pet stains, and no shed-snakeskin left lying around.... Nothing of that nature! Don't lose the perfect buyer who has a cat-allergic daughter.

● **(RED) Zoom** – Make sure your agent is contactable by Zoom, Skype, telephone, smoke signal – whatever it takes. If a buyer takes the time to contact your agent and there is no response, they will not always come back. If you've ever been house hunting, we've all experienced the agent who takes days to get back to you, or just forgets about you altogether. Even if it means you, or the buyer, have to leave a message before the agent gets back to you, at least a same day response is what you should be looking for.

You also need to be able to have the option of multimedia meetings with your agent. In a post-coronavirus world, virtual and Zoom viewings have become more and more important. Make sure your agent is tech-efficient!

Buyers decide in the first eight seconds of seeing a home if they're interested in buying it. Get out of your car, walk in their shoes, and see what they see within the first eight seconds

\- Barbara Corcoran

Join the team

You may be a salesperson, reading through this book, and thinking, "How can I do what Joshua Glanville is doing?"

Well, the modern approach to estate agency, that I keep referring to throughout the book, is something that we're able to implement with the help, training and the forward-thinking support of the fastest growing real estate brand in the world (as of 2020), eXp Realty.

eXp offers an unrivalled support system of other agents and their knowledge, as well as exceptional training, branding, and marketing advice. If you've ever wanted to be your own boss, eXp is the place to start. They have a framework for you to use in order to build your own brand, from the ground upwards to whatever heights you want to achieve.

If you want to start your own business, finally being able to have your ideal work/life balance, reaching heights you could only have dreamed of before, then get in touch so we can get you on board and set you up with the most exciting real estate movement in the world.

Contact me now on

- Phone: 020 8998 8009
- Email: joshua.glanville@exp.uk.com
- Instagram: @joshuaglanville
- Facebook: https://www.facebook.com/joshuaglanvilleproperty

About the author

JOSHUA GLANVILLE IS an award-winning estate agent, and a rapidly rising star in the real estate world. Born into a family of property developers, his passion for property started from a very young age. He was instrumental in building up the family's property business from a tiny farm building in the South of Italy to the multi-million pound property empire it is today.

Joshua trained as a lettings and sales negotiator at a local West London firm where, within two months, he was winning awards for being the company's top salesman, and was named the 'The One to Watch' in 2018.

Joshua's passion for business and property has taken him to three continents. He works alongside the esteemed Queensland property guru and property marketing expert, Lisa B, and is currently one of the only property experts in the UK who has this advanced marketing training. He also spent several months in the South of Florida studying US real estate models.

Joshua believes that his fresh approach to real estate is a sign of the times and is a sign of the future of real estate.

We are living in a time when digital and social media are everything. Gone are the days when agents can sit in their offices with photocopies of home details and a listing on Rightmove. People spend hours on their screens each day, which we have to recognise and jump in there with a full digital and social media marketing package.

This approach has served his clients well. As well as receiving the top lettings and sales negotiator awards over and over at his West

London high street agency, he has worked with developers to source multi million pound projects across London.

High Street estate agents to Joshua are the equivalent of the corner shop to Amazon.

www.ingramcontent.com/pod-product-compliance
Lightning Source LLC
Chambersburg PA
CBHW051005060726
47593CB00017B/1064